Puffin Books

FUN WITH PAPER MODELLING

Flying birds; puppets; piggy-banks; strange and fantastic monsters; mobiles and masks. If you just follow the fully illustrated, easy instructions in this book you can turn all sorts of things around the house – old newspapers, wire, balloons and soap – into a wide range of exciting and colourful toys and presents.

During the course of his teaching, G. C. Payne has been asked by many people for advice on how to model with paper and he has now put all his years of experience into this practical guide. Each stage is carefully explained and illustrated by over 100 drawings and 24 photographs and the methods can be easily adapted to suit your own individual needs.

Masks and Models for
Young People to Make

by G. C. Payne

Fun with Paper Modelling

Puffin Books

Puffin Books,
Penguin Books Ltd, Harmondsworth, Middlesex, England
Penguin Books Australia Ltd, Ringwood, Victoria, Australia
Penguin Books Canada Ltd,
41 Steelcase Road West, Markham, Ontario, Canada
Penguin Books (N.Z.) Ltd,
182–190 Wairau Road, Auckland 10, New Zealand
First published by Kaye & Ward 1966
Published in Puffin Books 1975
Reprinted 1975
Copyright © Kaye & Ward Ltd, 1966
Made and printed in Great Britain by Richard Clay (The Chaucer Press) Ltd,
Bungay, Suffolk
Set in Monotype Ehrhardt

Contents

Before You Start

This book shows a number of different ways of making paper models and masks. They can all be made quite easily and none of the materials needed are expensive or hard to get. In fact many of them can often be found around the house, for instance, newspaper, card from boxes, wallpaper paste, garden wire and balloons left over from Christmas or parties.

You will find ways of making masks which will be useful in plays or at times like Hallowe'en or Bonfire night, as well as decorations for parties and Christmas time or simply hanging on a wall.

Of course, they can also be made not for use but just for fun, because they *are* fun to make. The important thing is that they should be *your own* models and not just copied from the book. These illustrations are to show you how it is done and some uses for your work. *What* you make is something only you can decide. Use your imagination and the book will start you off on making something that is so much your own that only you could have made it.

If you follow the directions in each section, you should be successful with all your models, but remember that this sort of work can't be rushed. You must be patient and make sure that the model is quite ready before you go on to the next step.

Don't be afraid to try new things out. If you have an idea for altering or improving a model – try it! It may succeed or it may fail, but you should always be ready to experiment with your materials. It is only in this way that you will learn just what is possible and – even more important – what isn't.

One word of warning. It can be dangerous to cover your face completely with a mask. If you make masks on the lines suggested in this book they will be quite safe to wear, but *always*, before you put on a mask, make quite sure that it will be possible for you to breathe properly once it is on.

What You'll Need

These are the materials you will need for making the models in this book:

Clay	*Paste*	*Paints*	*String*
Paper	*Card*	*Varnish*	*Feathers*
Vaseline or Soap	*Wire*	*Muslin*	*Raffia*

Clay

For making moulds on which the paper models are formed, some sort of clay is needed. Either modelling clay or Plasticine can be used.

Modelling clay is cheap but unfortunately it shrinks as it dries and this can distort the model being made on it. One way of getting over this is to let the mould dry out completely before the paper is put on, but if you do this, remember to make the mould bigger than you wish the finished article to be to allow for shrinkage.

Plasticine is more expensive to buy but it may be used over and over again without any special preparation, and as it does not shrink, it is probably the best thing to use. If you find the Plasticine too hard to model easily, put it on a radiator or near a fire and it will soon become soft.

Paper

The success of all these models depends on the paper becoming hard as it dries. To make sure that this happens, you must see that the paper is well soaked with paste before it is put on. It is best to use a porous paper that will absorb plenty of paste.

Newspaper is good for general use, but avoid the slightly glossy paper used in many magazines. Do not use glossy 'art' paper at all. Blotting paper does the job very well. It is rather expensive if you use it in large quantities, but for a special model, particularly one that has to be light, it is worth the extra cost. Brown wrapping paper – not glossy – can be used for the first stages of large models.

Tissue paper is useful for the final covering of models and gives a good surface to paint on.

Vaseline or Soap

A thin layer of one of these should be put onto a clay mould before applying the paper, to prevent the paper sticking to the mould when it dries. Vaseline is probably the best thing to use, but if it is not available, soap and water made into a creamy liquid will do quite well.

Paste

Almost any cold-water paste can be used for this work. Though it does not perhaps dry quite so hard, cellulose adhesive of the sort used for wallpaper hanging does quite well. Avoid lumps in the paste and make it wet enough to soak into the paper rather than stay on the surface.

Card

When making these models, the opportunity arises to use up many scraps of card, and it is a good idea to have a box holding a collection of card pieces of different weights so that the right card can be selected for any particular job.

Generally speaking, card which is flexible and does not crease easily is the most useful. Scraps of hardboard and plywood should also be kept for possible use.

Wire

For making frames and armatures (the word used for a framework supporting a model), almost any type of wire may be used, although untreated steel wire is not satisfactory because the water in the paste will make the wire rust and in time this will show on the surface of the model.

Galvanized packing-case wire, which can often be obtained freely from factories and warehouses, is a good working base. Otherwise galvanized steel or aluminium wire can be bought by the pound from ironmongers.

Paints

Poster or powder colours will take quite well on the surface of these models. Emulsion paint is also suitable. All these paints are water based and water will soften the paste in the models and make them soggy. To avoid this, mix as little water as possible in the paint and work quickly. If it is necessary to put on a second coat, allow the model to dry out thoroughly first.

Varnish

Two or three coats of varnish will usually be required to give the model a glossy finish. Spirit varnish is probably the best as it does not change the colours underneath. Varnishing is not generally a good thing for theatrical use as it causes annoying reflections from stage lights.

Muslin

For joining together models which have been taken off the mould in halves, as well as for reinforcing the edges of models, bookbinding muslin cut into strips of $1'' - 1\frac{1}{2}''$ (25 mm–38 mm) is very useful. If you do not have this, surgical bandages of the same width will do equally well.

String, Feathers, Raffia, etc.

To make hair, moustaches and beards, or animals' manes and tails, etc., anything of this sort may be used. As with card, a box of assorted oddments of this type of material should be kept for use when needed.

Feathers are also very useful for decorating models, but they should be kept carefully in a separate box as they are so easily damaged.

Making Masks

To wear over your face

It is surprising what a difference putting on a mask makes to a person. When your face is covered up, and you look in the mirror and see something not like yourself at all, it makes you *feel* quite different.

If you are in a play and you really want to 'get into' the part you are playing, try making a mask of the character and see what a difference it makes. In addition to being made to fit particular characters in plays, masks can be highly imaginative, like the ones that witch doctors wear, or they can be accurate copies of animals or birds or fish as well as people.

Masks have been made for thousands of years by people all over the world and if you can find pictures of these in books, or, better still, go to a museum and see some real ones, you will get lots of ideas for making them yourself.

They can also be used for three-dimensional decorations. One or two of them hanging on a wall look very attractive.

Once you have made up your mind about what sort of mask you want to make, here is how to do it:

MATERIALS REQUIRED: *Board, Stiff Paper, Clay or Plasticine, Vaseline or Soap, Newspaper, Paste, Paints, Elastic*

First of all, find the size the mask must be in order to fit you. Take a piece of stiff paper, e.g. cartridge or sugar paper, and draw on it the outline of your face, checking the size and shape to make sure it will fit when finished. Remember to allow for shrinkage if you are going to use modelling clay for the mould.

Cut out the paper shape and put it on a rigid board such as a drawing board (Fig. 1). Now make a mould for the mask in clay or Plasticine on top of the paper shape (Fig. 2). The modelling

13

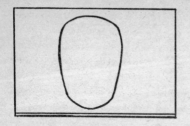

1. Paper pattern on board
2. Clay Mould
3. Section
4. Cover with paper strips
5. Remove model from board
6. Take clay out
7. Trim edges
8. Paint and fit elastic

should be carried out boldly and it is best to exaggerate the size of the nose, chin, lips and eyebrows.

Fig. 3 shows the sort of section of the mould you need in order to be able to get the mask off it easily when it is finished. Notice that there are no undercuts which will stop it from coming away.

When you are satisfied with the mould, clean up the edges with a knife or a pointed piece of wood, check that the mould is fitting the paper shape underneath and put a thin coating of Vaseline or liquid soap all over it.

Tear up a supply of paper strips. The strips should be fairly small, say 2″ × ½″ (50 mm × 13 mm), where they will have to fit over the features, but they can be larger on flatter surfaces. The best size of strip for any particular model will soon be found as you work. The important thing is that they should fit smoothly over the features without wrinkling or forming air pockets underneath.

Cover the strips of paper with paste. The paste must soak the paper thoroughly and you may need to leave them for a few minutes for this to take place.

Press the pasted strips onto the mould, gently smoothing them into position to take the shape of the features (Fig. 4). Do not press or rub too hard when doing this or it may spoil the shape of the mould underneath. Do not put all the strips lying in the same direction but place them criss-cross over each other as this will give a stronger result.

When the mould is completely covered with strips, go over it again and continue doing this until you have built up a thickness of 4–6 layers all over. Make sure that all parts of the mould are covered evenly. Though it is not necessary, it is a good idea to make the final layer of plain paper as this gives a better surface to paint on than newsprint.

The model must now be left until the paper covering is quite dry and hard. This may take several days. When you are quite sure it is ready, slip a knife under the edges of the model and lift it gently off the board with the clay still inside it (Fig. 5).

Loosen the paper from the clay by going round the edges and pulling it away. The mask should now come away from the mould quite easily (Fig. 6). If you do find it still sticking, take out some of the clay with a knife or spoon and try again.

Now trim the edges of the mask with a large sharp pair of scissors (Fig. 7), make holes in the eyes so that you can see through them, and a hole in the nose or mouth to breathe through, and it will be ready for painting. Put your paints on boldly, using them to emphasize the features, and use dark and light colours to give contrast. If you want the mask to be glossy or waterproof, varnish it when it is quite dry.

All that is needed now is an elastic strap to hold the mask onto your face. Punch a hole at each side, just above your ears and thread the elastic through these, holding it in place with knots (Fig. 8).

To wear on your head

Sometimes it is better to make a mask which does not fit over your face but covers the top of your head, leaving the face quite clear.

This sort of mask is shown in the inset (3b) and is very useful when the person wearing the mask has to speak or sing, as it does not muffle the voice at all.

The method of making this kind of mask is almost the same as that described on pages 13–16 and the same materials are used, but there are one or two differences.

1. The clay mould has to be made of the *top half of the head* instead of the face. The photograph in the inset (3a) shows a mould made in Plasticine ready for the strips to be put on.

2. As these masks are more comfortable to wear than those fitting actually over the face, they can be made stronger to last a long time and stand up to rough treatment. If you want a really sturdy mask, build up about 10 layers of paper on your mould.

3. These masks can be held in place on your head either by fitting a piece of elastic which goes under your chin or by adding a sort of hood, like the one in the photograph, which covers up all your head except the face.

To do this you need a square piece of cloth or felt (about 12″ × 12″, 30 cm × 30 cm). Sew the top edge of the material to the bottom back edge of the mask, using small stitches and strong thread, coloured to match the mask. When this is fixed in position, the mask may be put on and held in place by fastening the front edges of the hood together under the chin with a safety pin. You can make a neater finish by hemming the material and using a press stud for fastening. Once this hood is in position the mask will stay on your head very firmly and you can dance and run without any fear of it coming off.

How to add ears and horns

Both kinds of masks just described, as well as many that come later in this book, can be improved by the addition of extra features which cannot be made in the main body of the mask.

Remember – you must let the mask get quite dry and hard before putting them on.

Two of the most useful additions are ears and horns. Here is the way to make them:

Horns of complicated shape, like a stag's, are best made of strong cardboard. Cut out the horns in the shape you want them and then make a slot in the mask so that the base of the horn will fit into it (Fig. 1). Glue the horn into the slot and paste strips of paper all round the base to hold it in position (Fig. 2).

While the paste is wet the horn will not be rigid, so it should be put somewhere safe and the horn supported until the paste has hardened. Then the horn will be quite firm.

If the sort of horn you want to make is a round pointed one like a cow's or a rhino's, you can make it out of paper. Take a fairly large sheet of newspaper and cover it completely with paste. Now screw up the pasted paper and crumple and squeeze it into the shape you want (Fig. 3).

Put some paste on the mask in the place where you want the horn to fit and gently press the horn into position. Hold it in place with one hand while with the other you apply some strips of pasted paper to hold it firm (Fig. 4).

Finish the horn off by covering it with strips of paper, moulding it

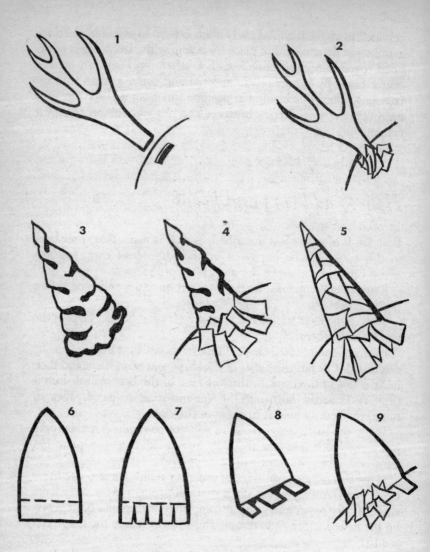

1. Slot to fit horn
2. Paper strips to hold it firm
3. Horn shape in pasted paper
4. Paper strips to hold it firm
5. Cover with paper
6. Cut ear out of card
7. Cut flange into tabs
8. Bend tabs
9. Fix with paper strips

into its final shape as you do so. If there are any large gaps or hollows in the surface of the horn, fill them up with small pieces of crumpled pasted paper before covering them over.

Ears are best made of card. Cut out the shape of the ear with an extra strip about $\frac{1}{2}''$ (13 mm) wide along the bottom (Fig. 6). This strip should now be cut into separate tabs (Fig. 7), and these bent in opposite directions alternately (Fig. 8).

The ear can now be put into position on the mask and held in place by means of strips of paper stuck over the tabs onto the ear and the main mask. A more even finish for painting can be obtained by covering the whole ear with paper strips.

Other features, for instance teeth and whiskers, can be added by the same method.

You can make a mask from a cardboard tube . . .

If you look at pictures of primitive tribes and the masks they wear for their ceremonies and dances, you will notice that often some of the dancers wearing masks look very tall and imposing. This is because they wear their masks on top of their heads like hats and under them they have long cloaks which cover their heads as well as their bodies. Eye-holes are cut in the cloak so that the wearer can see out.

These masks are great fun to make and to wear and can give even a small person a really impressive appearance. They can be made even more effective by covering over the eye- and mouth-holes in the mask with coloured cellophane and fixing up a small battery and bulb inside to make it light up. A switch may be carried in the hand and connected to the battery in the mask so that the light can be switched on and off at will.

Of course, the mask does not have to be worn in this way. It can be made big enough to slip right over your head and rest on your shoulders, when you can see through the eye-holes in the mask.

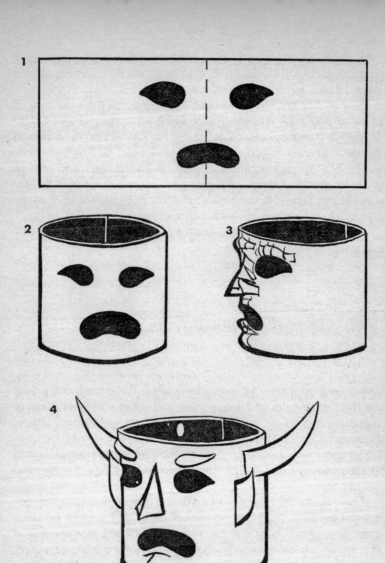

1. *Cut out eyes and mouth*
2. *Make into tube*
3. *Build up features*
4. *Add horns and ears*

20

You can make this type of mask, which is built up on a cardboard tube, in this way:

MATERIALS REQUIRED: *Strong but flexible Card, Glue, Newspaper, Paste, Paints, Feathers, Raffia, String, etc.*

You will need a rectangular piece of card as shown in Fig. 1. It should be about 12" (30 cm) high and wide enough to make a tube big enough either to fit round your head or rest comfortably on top, according to which fitting you are making. These measurements will be about 30" (76 cm) for the former sort and 24" (60 cm) for the latter.

Draw a line down the middle of the card and, using this as a guide, mark out the eyes and the mouth. Cut these out with a sharp knife (Fig. 1).

Make the card into a tube, being careful to bend it and not cause any creases. Overlap the ends by at least 1" (25 mm) and use staples, sewing, glue or adhesive tape to make a firm join (Fig. 2).

Now the mask is ready to have the features built up. This can best be done by first fastening the basic shape of the nose made in card to the mask and then completing the shape with strips and balls of pasted paper. Next make the eyebrow ridges and the lips in the same way and then build up the cheeks and the chin from pasted papers (Fig. 3).

The ears and horns can be made of flat card or of crumpled paper as described on pages 17–19. Remember that they may need supporting until they are dry and firm enough to remain rigid (Fig. 4).

Paint the mask in powder or poster colours. Do not try to be naturalistic in your painting, but use your imagination and be free with your patterns and colours, using them to heighten the effect of the features you have built up (Fig. 5). Once again it is a good idea to study the work of primitive peoples and see how wonderfully they have decorated their ceremonial masks.

Finish off the mask by adding feathers, string, raffia or wool to make the beard and the hair and the head-dress. Feathers may be painted or dyed in bright colours if handled with care and can be fixed in position on the mask by splitting the card with a sharp

21

5. Paint

knife and gluing them into place. If no feathers, raffia, etc. can be obtained, the decorations and beard can be made quite effectively from card, as shown in the inset (4).

. . . or on a wire frame

Sometimes you will want to make a mask to fit over your face and it will not be practicable to make it on a mould, because it has under-cuts, i.e. perhaps a continuation of the mask to fit under your chin, which would make it difficult to remove from the mould. Or it may be that the type of face you want to make a mask of is too deep to be removed satisfactorily from a mould. Animal heads are often of this kind. In these cases you can construct your mask on a wire frame.

You need a wire which can be easily bent and which is flexible enough to allow two pieces to be twisted together to make a join. It is surprising how strong a frame made of quite thin wire can be when it is made up. The sort of wire that is used for securing bales and parcels is very suitable for this work. For larger models the wire can be used double, twisted together to give extra strength.

As the strength of these models comes from the wire frame rather than from the paper covering, they can be made quite thinly, even as little as two layers of paper giving quite satisfactory results. Extra-light models can be constructed by using aluminium wire for the frame. Models made like this can be worn for long periods without discomfort.

MATERIALS REQUIRED: *Wire, Paper, Paste, Paints, Thread, Elastic*

Take a piece of wire about three feet (90 cm) in length and from it make a base frame of the right size to fit over your face with a little room to spare. It is important to allow this extra room as during the making of the mask the paper covering will be wrapped round the frame and use up some of the space inside. If you make this frame an exact fit to your face, the finished mask will be too small. Secure the ends of the wire by twisting them round each other (Fig. 1).

Add two wires running from top to bottom of the base frame. These will give the main shape of the mask and they should be bent exactly the same as each other into the correct shape for the animal represented (Fig. 2).

Take care when fastening the ends of wires by twisting them together to leave no sharp pieces sticking out as these can be dangerous. These ends should be bent to lie parallel with the frame so that they can be covered with paper later. If they are too stiff to be made to lie flat by hand, squeeze them into place with a pair of pliers.

Now add some pieces of wire to improve and fill out the shape of the mask and make the frame rigid (Fig. 3). Where the wires cannot be fastened together by twisting round the ends, hold them in place by tying with thread or thin wire.

Add two loops of wire for the ears (Fig. 4).

As you work on the frame you will probably find that some of the wires get pulled out of shape, so from time to time check the frame and make sure that the mask stays symmetrical and the base frame stays flat.

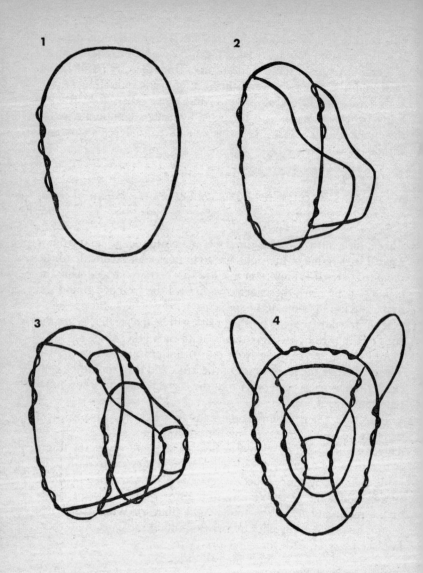

1. *Wire frame to fit face*
2. *Wires to give main shape*
3. *Bracing wires*
4. *Wire loops for ears*

24

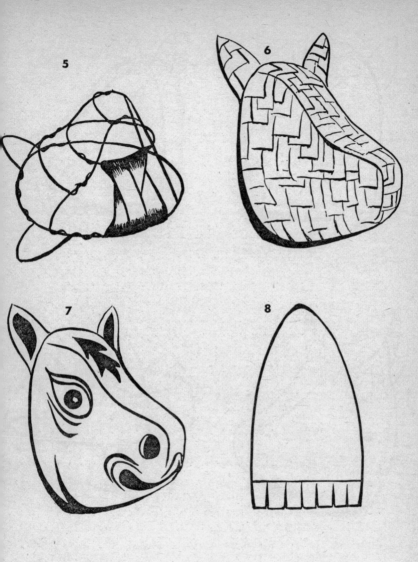

5. Cover with paper strips
6. Build up layers
7. Paint
8. Card shape for jaw

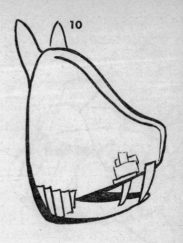

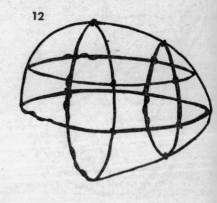

9. *Stick jaw on*
10. *Add teeth, cover joins*
11. *Add horns*
12. *Frame for whole head mask*

To start the paper covering, the first strips, soaked in paste, should be looped round the wires of the frame and stuck down (Fig. 5). Carry on adding more strips until the mask is completely covered and then build up the layers until the whole is covered with about four layers (less if a lightweight mask is required) (Fig. 6). Thin spots in the covering can be discovered by holding the mask up to the light.

When it has dried, and this may take two or three days, the paper will have become hard and the mask is ready for painting. Treat the painting in a broad, free manner, making the features stand out boldly (Fig. 7). Paint the backs of the ears as well as the fronts as they will be seen when the mask is worn.

An interesting way of improving this type of mask is to fix on a lower jaw made of card. First the shape of the lower jaw with an extra piece $1''-1\frac{1}{2}''$ (25 mm–38 mm) wide at the base is cut out of card (Fig. 8). This extra strip is cut into separate tabs and then fixed to the mask by bending the tabs over the mask frame and sticking them down (Fig. 9).

Paper strips stuck over the jaw and onto the paper covering of the mask will hold the jaw in position and cover the join. Teeth cut out of card may also be fixed on (Fig. 10).

If you need horns on your mask (Fig. 11), use either of the methods described on pages 17–19.

A mask to cover the whole of your head can be made by this method, but you will have to make the frame in the shape shown in Fig. 12. This is, of course, only a basic shape and you will have to change it to suit the particular mask you have in mind.

Cane can be used to make frames for this type of mask instead of wire, but it is not so easily shaped and all the joints will have to be tied. It is most useful for large masks which need to be kept light in weight.

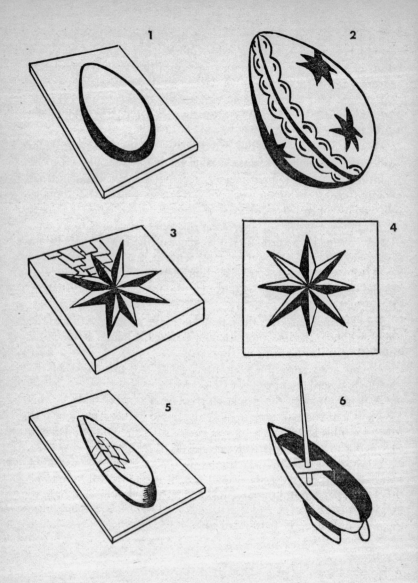

1. Mould for Easter egg
2. Completed egg
3. Mould for wall decoration
4. Finished decoration
5. Mould for boat hull
6. Finished boat

Making Models on Moulds

The method used for making a mask on a clay or Plasticine mould can be used for making a wide variety of models.

Here are some ideas for more models made in this way. You may be able to think of lots more for yourself.

An Easter egg

Make a mould for half an Easter egg (Fig. 1), build up layers of paper to make a model and take the model off carefully without damaging the mould. Now do the same again to make the second half. Stick a strip of thin card all round the inside of one half so that it projects about $\frac{1}{4}''$ (6 mm). This will enable you to join the two halves. Paint your egg, decorate it with 'glitter' or shapes cut from coloured foil, fill it with sweets and you have a wonderful present for someone (Fig. 2).

A wall decoration

Make a mould of a simple, bold three-dimensional design like the star shown in Fig. 3 and build up your paper model on it. You can cover the board it is made on also if you want to have your decoration made complete with its mounting (Fig. 4). Take the model off the mould, paint it in bright colours and hang it on a wall. You can build up a pattern of these by making several models and mounting them on a plywood or hardboard base.

A boat

Make the mould for the hull of the boat upside down on a board (Fig. 5).

Cover it with strips, take the model off the mould when dry and then put on the keel, rudder, masts, seats and sails which are made of card or paper (Fig. 6).

Historical ship models can be made in this way, as can models of present-day ships of all kinds. Make your hull with a flat bottom if you want it for a display, but if you want one which actually floats, weight the keel and give the hull three coats of varnish to make it waterproof.

NATURE STUDY SPECIMENS·

Models for nature study can be made from plaster casts of twigs, animals' footprints and specimens of all kinds.

Make your mould in the normal way. This gives you a 'negative' impression. Now make your model in the way described for the wall decoration and you will get a 'positive' impression which you can paint in natural colours. These lightweight models can easily be pinned up for display.

Models Made from Card or Wire

A fish on a flat card base

By using a combination of crumpled paper and paper strips, it is quite easy to build up a three-dimensional model of a fish using a piece of card as a base.

If the card is carefully cut out into the correct shape, an accurate model of any particular fish can be made which will be very suitable for use in displays of work in natural history.

Alternatively, the fish can be modelled in an imaginative way to make a gaily coloured model to be hung up or put into a group display in the form of an aquarium or an under-the-sea scene.

MATERIALS REQUIRED: *Stiff Card, Newspaper, Paste, Paint, Thin Card*

First cut the shape of the fish out of stiff card (Fig. 1). Thin card will warp and twist badly when the pasted paper is applied, and although a certain amount of bending helps to give a lively impression to the fish, too much will spoil the shape and make it difficult to make the model exactly how you want it.

Build up the bulk of the body of the fish by crumpling balls of pasted newspaper and putting them on to the card in the places where the fish's body bulges outwards. Do not use balls of paper which are too large as these will open out when applied to the card and will be difficult to cover smoothly.

Fix these crumpled balls in place by means of paper strips pasted over the top (Fig. 2).

Fig. 3 shows two different kinds of section you can build up for your fish. At the left is a model built up on one side only, leaving the other flat. This sort of model can be used for wall displays and for group pictures on a flat background.

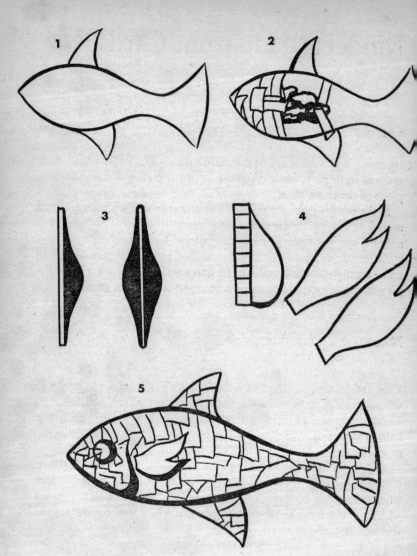

1. *Cut fish out of card*
2. *Build up shape*
3. *(Left) Section 1 (Right) Section 2*
4. *Gills and fins*
5. *Put together*

1. (a) Modelling materials.

Back row: inflated balloons, cold water paste powder, cellulose paste, egg trays. Front row: balloons, Plasticine, wire, clay, varnish, plain paper strips, newspaper.

(b) Working on a clay mould for a mask.

2. Full face masks. (see p. 13)

(a) *Clay mould for mask.*
(b) *Mask ready to be removed from mould.*

(c) *Mask made on a clay mould.*
(d) *Bird mask made on a clay mould.*

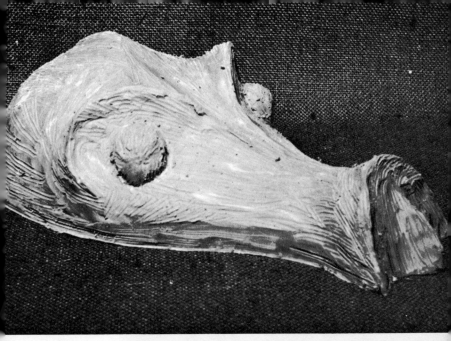

3. Masks to
wear on the
top of your
head.
(see p. 16)

(*a*) *Mould for
animal mask.*
(*b*) *Animal
mask completed.*

4. Card tube mask. (see p. 19)

5. (right) A mask on a wire frame. (see p. 22)

(*a*) *Starting to cover a wire frame mask.*
(*b*) *Completed wire frame mask.*

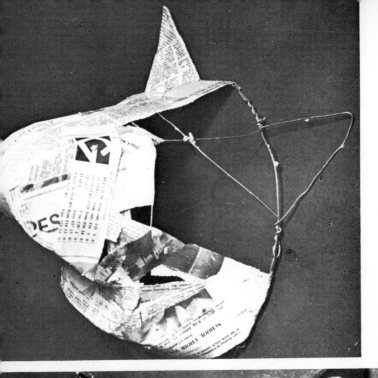

6–7. Models on a wire frame. (see pp. 37–40)

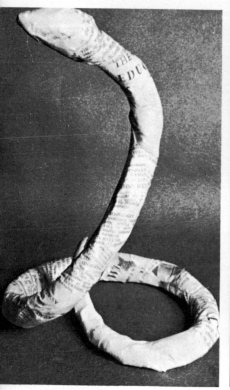

(a) *Building up a snake's body.*

(b) *Snake ready for painting.*

(c) Swan with card wings ready for painting.

8–9. Models
made on
balloons.
(see p. 41)

(a) *Putting the
first strips on to
a balloon.*
(b) *Pig ready for
painting.*

right :
(c) *Completed pig.*
(d) *A fish made on
a long balloon.*

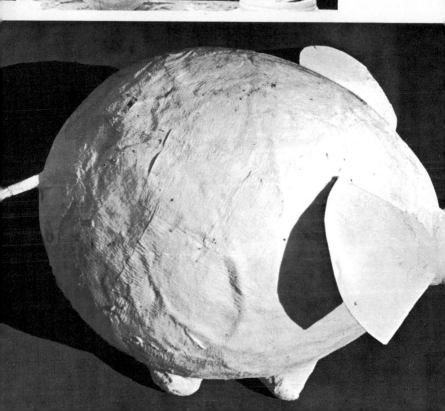

(a) *Halves of puppet head separated from the mould.*
(*see p.* 54)

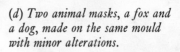

(b) *Eagle mask* (blotting paper), *ready for painting.*
(c) *Finished eagle mask.*

(d) *Two animal masks, a fox and a dog, made on the same mould with minor alterations.*

The right-hand section, built up on both sides, will give a fully three-dimensional model which can be mounted on a base or hung up.

Cut out the pectoral fins and gill plates from thin card, making tabs to secure them (Fig. 4), and fasten them to the model with paper strips. Build up the eye so that it protrudes slightly, cover the whole model completely with plain paper, e.g. kitchen paper or tissue, and the model is ready for painting.

Models built up on one side only, which are to be used in wall displays or pictures, need, of course, only be painted on one side. Varnishing on top of powder or poster paints will give a realistic appearance to the fish.

A fish on a built-up card base

For making larger models of fish, over about a foot (30 cm) in length, the method described on pages 31–3 is often not very satisfactory because it is difficult to stop warping in the card and the models tend to become rather heavy if made solid.

Here is a method useful for making large, yet rigid and light-weight models by making them hollow.

MATERIALS REQUIRED: *Stiff Card, Newspaper, Paste, Paint, Thin Card, Glue*

Cut out the body in two parts from stiff card. One part should be a typical fish shape including the tail if, as in most fish, this is vertical. The other part is cut in an oval shape, like a fish's body, but with no tail (Fig. 1). These two parts of the body are fitted together by means of slots, cut from the nose in the large piece and from the tail end of the smaller piece. Make the slots as wide as the card is thick and just long enough for the pieces to fit together with the noses in line. Do not make the slots too long or this will weaken the structure.

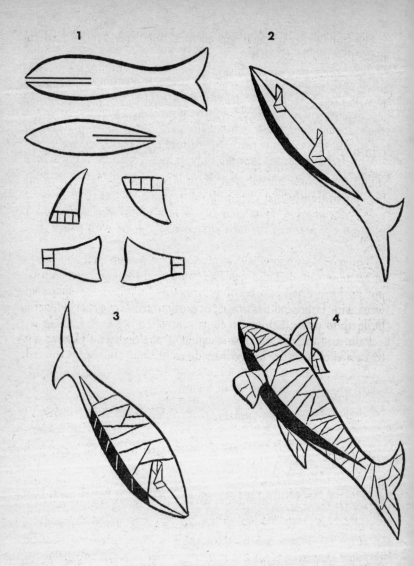

1. *Card shapes for base*
2. *Fix body together*
3. *Cover body*
4. *Fix fins, add eyes*

34

Cut out the dorsal, anal and pectoral fins from thinner card and make fixing tabs on each.

Put strong glue on the inside of each slot and holding the small piece horizontally and the larger piece vertically, slide the two parts together until the correct position is reached. Make the frame quite rigid by fixing small flanged triangular pieces of card as shown in Fig. 2. The larger the model you are making, the more of these reinforcing pieces you will need and the larger they should be.

Now start covering the body by winding strips of pasted paper round the frame (Fig. 3). Put them on tightly enough not to sag, but not so tightly that they pull the frame out of shape.

When you have completed two layers of paper, fix the fins in position by means of the tabs and cover the joins with paper strips (Fig. 4).

The model will now have a rather square section so if you want it to be more rounded and fish-like, wait until the two layers already put on have dried and become firm, then build up the shape you want with crumpled pasted paper and strips. The eyes can also be built up to make them more conspicuous.

Paint and varnish your model when it has dried out and hang it up by means of threads through the dorsal fin and the top of the tail.

A bird in flight can be made this way too

The method of making a bird is very similar to that for making the fish on pages 33-5. Very large models with wing spans of up to four feet (120 cm) can be made like this. They look most effective hanging from the ceiling on threads or wires and they may, if mounted on thin sticks or stiff wires, be used for shadow puppets.

MATERIALS REQUIRED: *Stiff Card, Newspaper, Paste, Paints, Thin Card, Glue*

Cut the two parts of the body and the wings out of the stiff card (Fig. 1). Unlike the fish, in this case the piece with the tail is the

1. Card shapes for base
2. Assemble body and wings
3. Cover body
4. Add crest and eyes

36

part to be held horizontally when slotting the two together. Cut the slots as for the model of the fish, taking particular care when cutting the slot through the beak. A very sharp knife and a steel ruler should be used for this to ensure that it is done accurately.

Cut the crest, with tabs at the bottom, out of thin card.

Glue the two parts of the body together, putting in sufficient strengthening triangles to make it rigid and then stick the wings on to the horizontal part of the body frame (Fig. 2).

Cover the frame with strips of pasted paper (Fig. 3). At the point where the wings join the body, build the paper into smooth curves so that the wings seem to grow naturally from the body. Take particular care with covering the head and the beak as the shape of these is rather complicated and needs many narrow strips rather than a few wide ones. If you cover the wings with a layer of paper strips, the 'pull' of the paste as it dries will give them a rather interesting natural curve, but try to make sure that you treat each wing exactly the same or they will twist by different amounts and look a little odd.

Fix the crest on by its tabs, cover the join with strips and make the body section round instead of square if you prefer this (Fig. 4). Build up the eyes slightly and paint the model in gay, bright colours.

Hang it in an interesting flying attitude – climbing, diving, banking or gliding – you will find that the shape the wings have taken up will help you to choose the best position for your particular model.

Make a lifelike snake . . .

The mask on pages 22–7 was made by sticking a covering of paper over a wire framework, but for many models of animals it is better to make them solid by building up the bulk of the body, legs, etc., on a suitably shaped wire frame. By this method, models of up to two feet (60 cm) in length can be made quite easily and quickly.

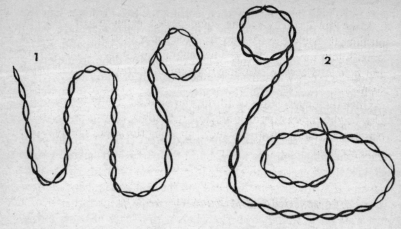

1. Wire armature for snake   *2. Another shape for snake armature*

Perhaps the simplest model to start with is a snake. Here is how to set about it:

MATERIALS REQUIRED: *Wire, Newspaper, Paste, Paints, Card*

Twist two lengths (about 15″, 40 cm) of wire together to make the body of the snake and at one end make the wire into a circle for the head. It is better to use two pieces of thin wire in this way than to have one thick piece, as the twists enable you to get a start with the paper covering more easily. Once the wires are firmly together, bend them into a suitable shape as in Figs. 1 and 2. Try to make a shape which gives an appearance of movement, but do not make any of the bends too sharp or you will have difficulty in building up the body satisfactorily. Try to imagine the thickness of the snake's body as you bend the wire so that you can visualise the finished animal.

Now spread paste on some long strips of paper about 1″ (25 mm) wide and wind them round the body. Continue doing this until you have built up the body to the right thickness. Make the body taper gradually to a point at the tail and keep the surface as smooth as possible as you work.

Make the head by rolling some pasted paper into a ball and pushing it inside the wire circle. Cover it with strips and make a smooth join on to the body. The tongue should be cut out of card and held in place by covering the bent-over end with small paper strips.

Once the paper is dry and firm, the model is ready for painting. Use bright contrasting colours and remember that on a snake the patterns are more effective if they run along the snake's body rather than across it.

... *prehistoric animals or a zoo*

Once you have successfully made a snake, you should be able to tackle other wire frame models. The drawings on pages 39 and 40 show some ideas for frames for these. Of course there are many more models you can make and you will probably want to think out your own ways of making a frame for the particular creature *you* want to make.

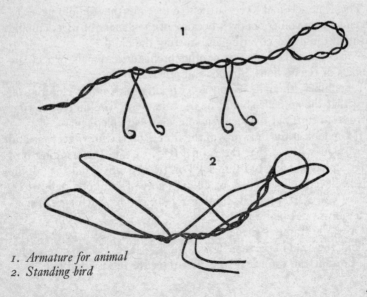

1. Armature for animal
2. Standing bird

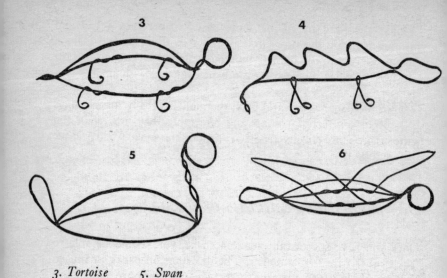

3. Tortoise   5. Swan
4. Lizard   6. Bird in flight

These models make very attractive toys but they should never be given to very young children because of the danger of wires coming through the paper covering and hurting the child.

You could make dinosaurs or other prehistoric animals, or accurate models of tigers, lions, giraffes and other animals.

Remember, though, if you are working with other children on this, that the animals should be to scale – you wouldn't want your tortoise to turn out bigger than someone else's elephant!

If you look at the drawings of the frames on the previous page and above you will see that the animal (Fig. 1), and the standing bird (Fig. 2), have bodies built up solid on twisted wires, but that all the others have hollow bodies made on a sort of cage of single wires. Before you start a model, think carefully about which sort of construction would be best for it.

Once the frame is made, you simply cover it with paper strips, making the head in the same way as for the snake. Horns, crests, etc., can be added in the usual way after the covering is complete.

Models Made on Balloons

Animals

In all the models we have dealt with so far, we have had to make our own mould or framework upon which the paper model is built. This section deals with models made on ready-made moulds which can easily be obtained in a wide variety of shapes – balloons.

At first sight it seems almost impossible that a firm, strong model could be built on such a flimsy thing as a balloon, but in fact, if you once try it, you will find that the use of balloons offers tremendous possibilities for a large number of different models which are not only rigid and strong, but also very light in weight.

Suppose you start by making an animal. Here is what to do:

MATERIALS REQUIRED: *Balloon, Newspaper and Kitchen Paper, Paste, Card, Paint, Egg Trays, Ice-Cream Cups, String*

Blow up the balloon fairly hard so that it does not press in very much when you touch it with a finger. Seal it either by tying a knot in the neck or by knotting thread or string round it. The knot in the neck makes the best seal, but it is more difficult to release later (Fig. 1).

Coat the balloon with a thin layer of Vaseline or liquid soap so that it may easily be taken out of the model later. In fact, the balloon can often be removed without this coating, but occasionally it will stick and damage the inside of the model, so it is worthwhile taking the trouble to put the coating on.

Cover the surface of the balloon, except for a piece about 1″ (25 mm) in diameter around the neck or valve, with strips of paste-soaked paper. These should be large enough to allow the covering to be done quickly, but not so large that they wrinkle as they are put on. Strips of about 4″ × 1″ (100 mm × 25 mm) will be found suitable for most balloons (Fig. 2).

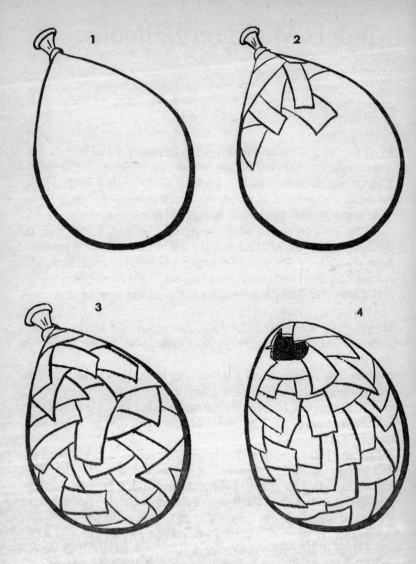

1. *Blow up balloon*
2. *Cover with paper strips*
3. *Build up 4–6 layers*
4. *Remove balloon*

Continue building up the covering until the whole balloon, except for the area round the valve, has five layers all over it (Fig. 3). It is important that the covering should be of even thickness all over to prevent weak spots, so it is a good idea to do alternate layers of different papers, say one layer of newspaper, the next of kitchen paper and so on. In this way you can see at a glance when one layer is complete and it is time to start the next.

Once the covering process is finished, put the model on a piece of paper to prevent it sticking to the table or work-bench, and leave it to dry. Quicker drying may be obtained by hanging the balloon up by means of a string round the valve, but *do not* put it near a fire or radiator to dry as this will cause the air inside to expand and eventually burst the balloon, spoiling the model.

When the model is quite dry and firm, untie the neck of the balloon and release the air inside it. When deflated, it may be withdrawn through the hole left in the paper layers (Fig. 4).

Balloons taken out of models may be used several times on different models before they become useless.

If you have difficulty in removing the balloon, leave it inside the model rather than risk damaging the paper layers. It will do no harm if you tuck the valve inside the model so that a smooth surface is left outside.

With more strips of paper soaked in paste, make several layers of paper over the hole where the balloon came out of the model so that the surface is rounded and complete (Fig. 5).

Now take a good look at the model, trying to see what possibilities it offers for making into an animal. Try it in several positions, on end, on its side and so on and see what it suggests to you. The shape of the balloon shown in the drawings, when placed on its side, is very suggestive of a pig, so that is the model we will see how to complete.

The first step towards completion is to put on the legs. These can be made of crumpled paper covered over and joined on to the body with paper strips (Fig. 6), but an easier way, for a model with short legs like this one, is to use sections from papiermâché egg trays, covering and attaching them in the usual way.

If you are making an animal with longer legs, roll up into a tube a sheet of fairly stiff paper covered in paste. Fasten this to the body

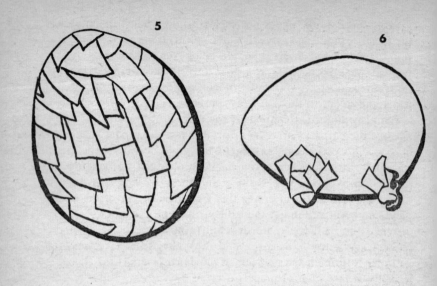

5. *Cover valve-hole*
6. *Add legs*
7. *Add ears, tail and snout*
8. *Paint*

of the model with paper strips and complete the covering and modelling of the legs when they have dried and hardened into position.

The snout can be built up in the same way from crumpled paper – or again there is an easy way. This time use an ice-cream cup and cover and fix it with paper strips.

Ears cut from card may be made and attached in the usual way (see page 19), and a tail made of string fixed on by fraying the end and sticking strips over the fibres to hold it in place. The method described on pages 17–19 may also be used for putting on horns, tusks, teeth, etc.

Paint the model when it is dry and firm all over. With this type of model it is very important to do the painting quickly, putting very little pressure on the brush as you work so that the model does not become soggy or dented due to the effect of the water in the paint. Varnishing will give a glossy, waterproof finish, but you will probably find that more than one coat is needed.

This model could be made into a piggy-bank by cutting a slot for coins in the top using a sharp knife. It will be necessary to cut a hole in the bottom in order to empty it later, but the piece need not be completely removed. Leave it attached at one side and re-seal it with adhesive tape after the box has been emptied.

Of course this is only one possibility for an animal made on one particular shape of balloon. In the next few pages we will see that a great variety of models can be made on different balloon shapes.

Birds and fishes

Many shapes of balloon lend themselves to making birds and fishes. Their rounded shapes and smooth contours are the ideal base for the development of models of this kind.

However, it is a mistake to decide firmly what sort of creature you are going to make too early on. The best way to go about it is always to complete the basic shape on your balloon first and then let this suggest ideas to you. Hold it, examine it and run your hands over it.

45

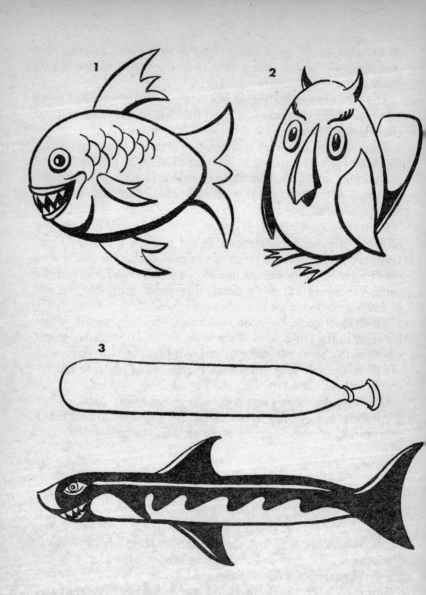

1. *A fish*
2. *An owl*
3. *A shark on a long balloon*

Look at it from all angles and finally make your mind up only when you are satisfied that you have the best possible answer for the particular shape you have.

Of course, sometimes it may be necessary for you to start off with a particular creature in mind. For instance, you might need a model of a shark for a shadow puppet play or a geography display. In that case you should choose your shape of balloon very carefully so that the model can be built up on it in a natural way. This sort of job apart though, it is much more fun to start with the shape and get the idea from that rather than the other way round.

The drawings opposite show you some of the ways in which balloons can be made into birds or fishes. The fish (Fig. 1), and the owl (Fig. 2), are both made on round balloons with additions in card. On the fish the fins and tail are made of card and fastened by means of tabs (see page 18). The eyes are simply circles of card stuck on and the rest is done by painting. The features of the owl are made in exactly the same way but the feet are made of much stiffer card so that the model will not tip over. The beak and the ears may, if you prefer it, be built up solid, in the way described for making horns on pages 17–19, instead of being made of card.

For the shark model in Fig. 3 the basic long balloon shape has to be modified quite a lot at the nose and the tail to get the necessary shape. The nose can be built up while the model is still on the balloon, but fix the card tail into the gap after removing the balloon and then finish off the modelling around this. You could make very striking looking teeth by using white painted sunflower or marrow seeds stuck into position with strong glue.

Dragons and other fabulous beasts

The more models of this kind you make, the more possibilities seem to present themselves for development into exciting new creations. Balloons can be obtained in a wide variety of shapes and sizes and all of them offer possibilities for models which may be naturalistic and based on some known creature or quite imaginary, producing a fantastic beast completely of your own invention.

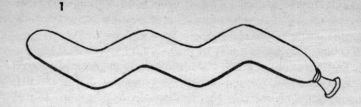

1. *This balloon –*
2. *– can become a snake –*
3. *– or a dragon*

48

Take the balloon shown in Fig. 1 for instance. The shape of this immediately suggests a snake and Fig. 2 shows how easily, with the addition of a rounded head, a tongue and a pointed tail, this can be done. But why stop there? The addition of a crest and a spiky tail, together with legs ending in sharp claws, all made of card, can transform this into an impressive dragon (Fig. 3).

Even this is not the end. You could add wings and horns and make it into an even more fabulous beast. The way you paint it can also make a great difference. Look at paintings of monsters and dragons in books and art galleries and notice how the colours are used to make them even more dreadful and frightening, then see if you can get the same sort of effect with your paints.

Fig. 5 shows how another shape of balloon can be made into a fantastic animal. Notice how a long tail made of card and built up in thickness with paper strips has been added and how the bulges in the balloon have been used to provide mountings for the legs and the spines along the back.

Party Decorations

Balloons can also be used to make very attractive decorations for use at home or at school for Christmas or a party. Any shape of balloon can be used and one of the advantages of using these for decorations is that although they can be made quite large, they are very light in weight so that they are easy to hang. Ordinary sewing thread, which is almost invisible in use, will easily support one of these so that it seems to float in mid-air.

When making them, it is a good idea to fasten a loop of string for hanging at the top of the balloon. Do this at the time when you are building up your layers of paper, holding down the ends of the string by pasting paper strips over them.

Fig. 6 shows a decoration made on a round balloon. It could be painted and then varnished to make it shiny, or it could be covered all over with aluminium cooking foil and other shapes put on top cut from coloured foil. A good way of fixing these foils on to the paper shape is to fasten them by means of a staple gun.

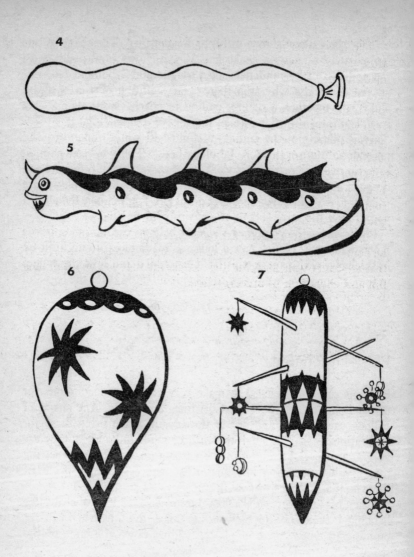

4. *This queer shaped balloon –*
5. *– can become an even queerer creature*
6. *Decoration made on a round balloon*
7. *Decoration made on a long balloon*

50

The decoration in Fig. 7 has been made on a long balloon and after painting, wooden dowels have been pushed through holes made with a sharp pointed awl. Decorative shapes cut from card and painted gaily or covered with foil, have then been hung on threads from the ends of the dowels.

Easter eggs can be made on balloons. Use a suitably sized egg-shaped balloon, build up your layers of paper, and when it is dry and hard, take out the balloon. If you want to fill it with sweets or a gift, cut it into two with a very sharp knife. Stick a strip of card 1" (25 mm) wide inside one half with about ¼" (6 mm) projecting all round so that the other half will fit on to it, and your Easter egg is ready for painting.

Remember that all these are only examples to show you what can be done. Make sure you set about designing and constructing models that are really your own, for it is in this way that you will find most fun and enjoyment in making them.

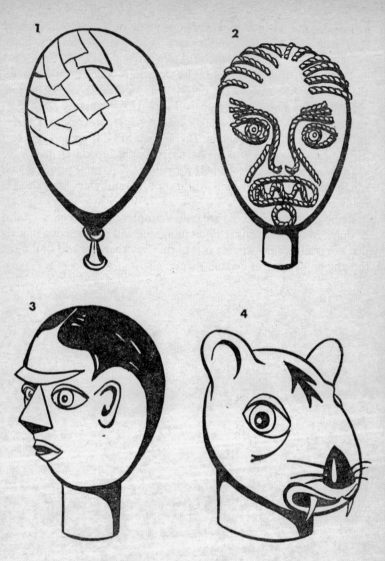

1. *Cover balloon with strips*
2. *Outline features in string –*
3. *– or model them in card*
4. *An animal head*

Puppet Heads

Made on a balloon . . .

If you look at the shape of an ordinary round balloon, you will see that its shape resembles that of a head, the narrow part where the valve is being the chin and the rounded end the top of the head. This provides an opportunity to make a puppet head which can be used in different ways. If a tube of card of the correct diameter is built on during the making (Fig. 2), a stick like a broomstick can be fixed inside it, cloth tied round it like a cloak, and the model used as a kind of rod puppet. A wider tube, as in Figs. 3 and 4 enables a hand to be put inside and the puppet manipulated in this way. Once again, a covering of cloth should be attached to conceal the hand and arm of the user.

MATERIALS REQUIRED: *Balloon, Newspaper, Paste, Card, Paint*

Choose a balloon of the right size for the puppet you want to make, blow it up and cover it in the way described on pages 41–43 (Fig. 1). Take out the balloon when the paper is dry and cover the valve-hole. Now the features can be added. A quick way of doing this is shown in Fig. 2. The features are outlined in string, using different thicknesses if necessary, sticking them down with strong glue. Paint the head, leaving the string unpainted at first. When the rest of the painting is complete, pick out the string in contrasting colours. Gold or silver metallic paint is very effective for this.

Another way is to model the features in card (Fig. 3), giving a final covering of paper all over to make a uniform surface for painting.

Hair, beard, moustache, etc., can be made of string, raffia or wool.

The same shape of balloon is suitable for making animals' heads (Fig. 4). Here again the features can be modelled in card or outlined in string before painting. Stiff bristles from a sweeping brush make good whiskers for these animal heads.

. . . or on a mould

This method can be used for making puppet heads of all types – shadow puppets, rod puppets, glove puppets or string-operated puppets. You can make them any size you require, from life-size or even larger down to tiny ones only an inch (25 mm) in diameter. However big they are, the method remains the same, but great care is needed with the very small ones, especially in making the mould and putting on the covering, for they can soon become shapeless if the modelling is not crisply done and the covering not put on neatly without any wrinkles.

For a first attempt, a suitable size would be a model about six inches (15 cm) high.

MATERIALS REQUIRED: *Clay or Plasticine, Newspaper, Paste, Paints, String, Raffia, Wool, etc.*

Make the clay or Plasticine model, trying to fit the face to the character you are trying to portray. Model the features strongly – exaggerate them a little – it is all to the good in this sort of job (Fig. 1).

When the mould is finished, cover it with a layer of liquid soap or Vaseline and start to cover it with strips of paper soaked in paste. You will find that quite small strips are needed, especially over the features, to avoid wrinkling and distortion of the shapes (Fig. 2). After five or six layers have been built up (Fig. 3), allow the paper covering to dry and become quite hard.

Removing the model from the mould presents a difficulty as the shape of the head will not allow it to be pulled straight off.

It is possible to scoop out the clay from the inside of the model with a spoon (if it is still soft), but this is not very satisfactory as it sometimes damages the model or leaves clay inside. A better

54

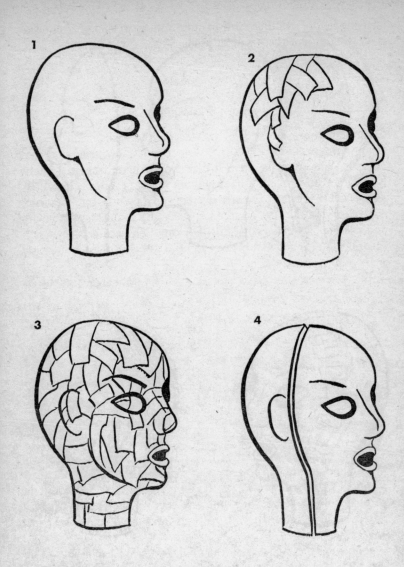

1. Clay mould
2. Stick on strips
3. Build up 4–6 layers
4. Cut in half when dry

55

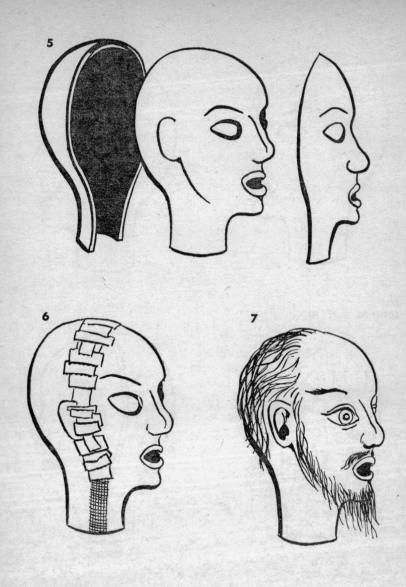

5. *Take model off mould*
6. *Join halves*
7. *Add hair and beard. Paint*

56

method is to cut the model into two pieces for removal. With a sharp-pointed knife, make a cut all round the model as shown in Fig. 4. The two halves will now separate from the mould quite easily (Fig. 5). With a few minor repairs, the mould could now be used again for another model head.

The two halves have now to be joined together again. This is best done by fixing them roughly together with paperclips at the neck and an elastic band round the head. Then stick a strip of muslin or surgical bandage about 1″ (25 mm) wide over the join, making sure that the edges are accurately put together. Stick paper strips over the top to strengthen the join and cover the muslin. Trim the edges at the neck to make a neat, level bottom, then paint the model and varnish it if you want it to be glossy.

The hair, beard, etc., which may be made of string, raffia, wool or any other suitable material, can be added when the varnish has dried (Fig. 7). The head can now be fixed on to a wooden body with glue, or if it is a glove puppet you are making, the clothes can be sewn on at the neck.

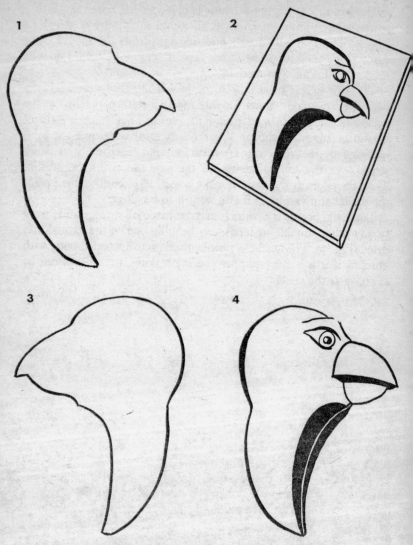

1. Cut template from stiff paper
2. Model half-head on template
3. Reverse template for second half-head
4. Put halves together to finish modelling

Whole Head Masks

Method 1. A two-piece mould

Now that you are experienced in the skills of mask and model construction, you are probably ready to master the more difficult process by which a whole head mask can be made.

There is no doubt that the masks produced by this method are the most effective of all as they consist of a model of the whole of the animal or bird's head, which goes on top of the wearer's head, and a helmet which fits round the face, leaving it clear for taking part in drama, singing or poetry speaking.

MATERIALS REQUIRED: *Modelling Board, Clay or Plasticine, Stiff Paper, Newspaper or Blotting Paper, Vaseline or Liquid Soap, Paste, Paints, Card*

Make a profile drawing of the mask you are going to make (Fig. 1). This should be done on stiff paper such as cartridge paper. The size of this profile must be correct. The upper part – the animal's head – can be as big as you like, but the lower part – the helmet – must be the right size to fit your head.

Cut out the pattern, or template as it is called, and place it on a modelling board. Then build up a half-mould of the mask on it, making sure that the mould fits exactly on the template (Fig. 2). Notice how the cut-out in the helmet for the face is made on this half-mould, and be sure to make this the right size for your face to fit into when the two halves are put together.

Now take the mould off the drawing board, being careful not to damage it, and remove the template. Turn this over so that it is reversed on the drawing board to make the second half of the mould on (Fig. 3). Model the second half, trying to make it the exact mirror image of the first.

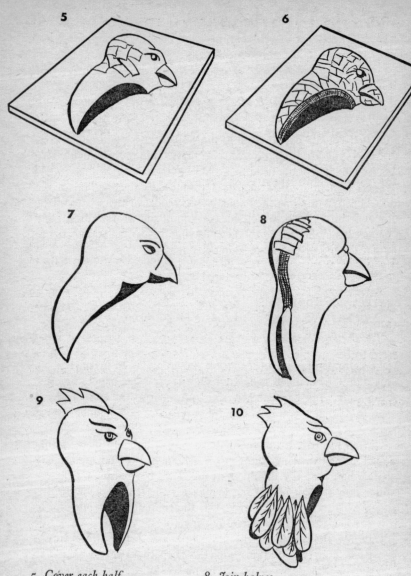

5. Cover each half
6. Trim and reinforce edges
7. Remove model from mould

8. Join halves
9. Add crest
10. Paint, add neck feathers

The best way to finish the modelling and make sure that the two halves fit exactly is to put them together, holding them in place with wide rubber bands that are not too tight (Fig. 4). It is a good plan to leave the paper template on the second half while this is being done as it will help the halves to separate easily.

When you are satisfied with the modelling and symmetry of the mould, separate the halves and put each one down on a board. Cover them with layers of pasted paper strips (Fig. 5). If you use newspaper, you will need five or six layers, but if you decide on blotting paper, which, giving a very light result, is most suitable for this work, two layers will be enough.

When the paper layers have dried, trim all the edges with a sharp knife. At this time, if you want it, you can make a cut-out at the back of the helmet, to make it easier to put on. Reinforce all edges with muslin strips about 1″ (25 mm) wide (Fig. 6). The models can now be taken off the mould (Fig. 7), and joined with another strip of muslin which is afterwards covered with paper strips (Fig. 8).

Attach any features such as crest, horns, ears, etc., which may be necessary. These can be made of card or crumpled pasted newspaper (see pages 17–19).

Try the mask on now and see if there are any alterations which need to be made to make the helmet fit comfortably. Use a large, sharp pair of scissors for this. After painting, the appearance of many animal masks may be improved by the addition of whiskers made from stiff broom bristles.

Method 2. A one-piece mould

This is a quicker, rather easier way of making a whole head mask like the one overleaf. However, it has one or two drawbacks: the helmet is not as complete as in the first method and needs to have either a piece of cloth attached at the bottom or a piece of elastic fitted to hold the mask in place on your head; also there is a limit to the size the model can be made before the clay sags. However, if you do have a mask to make where these points are not important, you will find this method worth adopting.

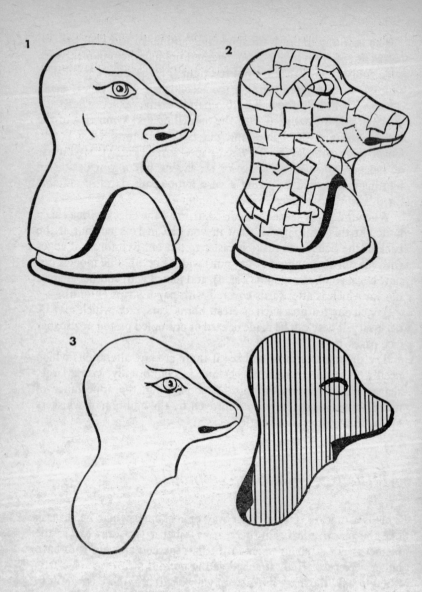

1. *Make mould on bowl*
2. *Build up paper layers*
3. *Cut model in half, remove from mould*

62

Materials required are the same as for method 1 on pages 59–61 except for the addition of a rounded bowl the same size as your head. First model the helmet round the bowl, and then build the head of the mask on top of this.

Cover the whole mould with newspaper or blotting paper strips. When dry, cut the model into two halves with a very sharp knife so that it can be removed from the mould. Trim the edges of the helmet and reinforce them with strips of muslin. From now on, do the same as in method 1 to complete the work.

More Ideas for Paper Modelling

We have reached the end of this book, but it is certainly not the end of what you can do in paper modelling. Once you know the methods, you are sure to find all sorts of occasions to use them in many different ways.

Most of the models in the book have been small in size, but there is almost no limit to the size they can be made. The 'big heads', for instance which are often seen in carnivals and parades, can be made on a frame. Of course, wire will not be strong enough and you will have to make your frame of wood and wire netting, but apart from that, the methods are just the same – only on a bigger scale.

In the same way, life-sized figures can be made. You could make a knight in armour for history, perhaps, or a life-sized model of a tiger for work in geography – all you need is the courage to make a start and a determination to solve the problems as they arise.

Pictures in relief, quite small or very large indeed, can also be made in paper. Use insulation board or hardboard as your base, build up the bulk of your model with egg trays, and used crumpled pasted paper and paper strips to complete the detailed modelling and the covering. These relief pictures are very useful in all sorts of displays and exhibitions, as they give a three-dimensional effect, yet can be fixed flat on a wall or screen.

Another interesting project is to make a pantomime dragon or some other animal to use in plays or parades. The open-bottomed frame is again made of wood and wire netting and this is covered with pasted paper – brown paper would be best in this case. The frame should be made big enough for two or more people to get inside it and shaped so that they can take the weight on their shoulders.

Television, films and books often show pictures of models made using techniques described in this book. Whenever you see one, try to decide which method was used to make it and see if you can adapt it to your own purposes.

Always remember though, whatever you do, *to make your own models*, not just copies of someone else's.